LEARN TO PLAY...

PIANO · VOCAL · GUITAR
AUDIO DEMO – SONG LESSON

★★★ SOMEONE LIKE YOU ★★★

PLUS 15 MORE GREAT SONGS

This is the brand new way
to learn to sing and play the
songs you love!

LEARN TO PLAY...

SOMEONE LIKE YOU

PLUS 15 MORE GREAT SONGS

PIANO VOCAL GUITAR
AUDIO DEMO – SONG LESSON

WISE PUBLICATIONS
part of The Music Sales Group

London / New York / Paris / Sydney / Copenhagen /
Berlin / Madrid / Hong Kong / Tokyo

Published by

WISE PUBLICATIONS
14-15 Berners Street, London W1T 3LJ, UK.

Exclusive Distributors:

MUSIC SALES LIMITED
Distribution Centre, Newmarket Road,
Bury St Edmunds, Suffolk IP33 3YB, UK.

MUSIC SALES CORPORATION
180 Madison Avenue, 24th Floor,
New York NY 10016, USA.

MUSIC SALES PTY LIMITED
Units 3-4, 17 Willfox Street, Condell Park,
NSW 2200, Australia.

Order No. AM1008623
ISBN: 978-1-78305-501-2
This book © Copyright 2014 Wise Publications,
a division of Music Sales Limited.

Compiled and edited by Jenni Norey.
Cover design by Fresh Lemon.
Printed in the EU.

THE A TEAM

Ed Sheeran

Singer-songwriter Ed Sheeran wrote 'The A Team' after playing a gig at a homeless shelter. Released in June 2011, it became the best-selling debut single of that year and found its way onto Sheeran's first album, +. Despite the serious subject, this song has quite a hopeful and uplifting feel.

The four-bar introduction emulates the acoustic guitar sound from the original recording, so play it with a light touch; note that the right hand is in the bass clef for this section:

This arrangement has the vocal melody incorporated into the right hand part, making it appear visually quite complex. Don't be put off by this as it really isn't so tricky, especially with the nicely simplified left hand part to help keep you on track. A good way to learn this song would be to ignore the lower part of the right hand until you feel confident playing the melody over the left-hand bass notes, like this:

Once mastered, you can start to add the right hand harmonies to fill the song out.

THE A TEAM

Words & Music by Ed Sheeran

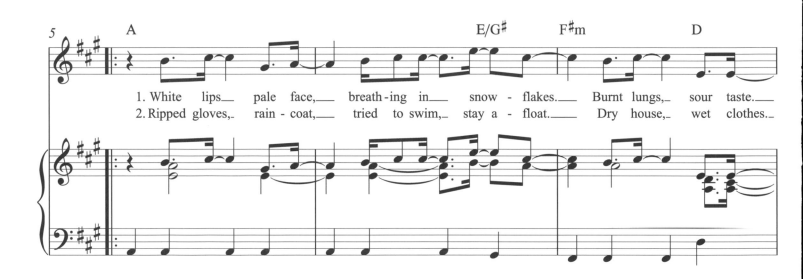

12

FEELING GOOD
Muse

This is Muse's version of the Leslie Bricusse and Anthony Newley song, originally written for the 1964 musical *The Roar Of The Greasepaint – The Smell Of The Crowd*. A classic, this song has been covered by many diverse artists over the years including Nina Simone and Michael Bublé. Muse's 2001 cover is regarded as one of the best and has been used prominently in TV advertising, drama and film.

This song has been arranged without the melody in the right hand and provides a full and realistic accompaniment for the singer. The structure is quite repetitive but dynamic contrasts will help get across the different feelings of the verses. Use the sustain pedal to hold down all the notes in bar 1. Keep the volume right down until bar 12 at which point you can really hit the keys hard!

Keep the level high through the second verse until the second time bar where you should drop back down to the original level before hitting bar 24 hard for the last verse and into the coda. Bar 32, where the right hand switches to playing broken chords, sees another sudden drop in volume which lasts to the end of the song:

FEELING GOOD

Words & Music by Leslie Bricusse & Anthony Newley

(Play cue notes 2nd and 3rd time)

1. Birds fly - ing high,_____ you know how I feel.__
2. Fish in the sea,_____ you know how I feel.__
3. Stars when you shine,_____ you know how I feel.__

Sun in the sky,_____ you know how I feel. Reeds__
Riv - er run - ning free, you know how I feel.
Scent of the pine,_____ you know how I feel. Now

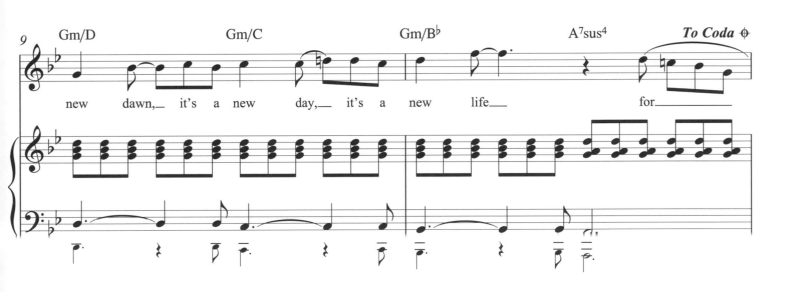

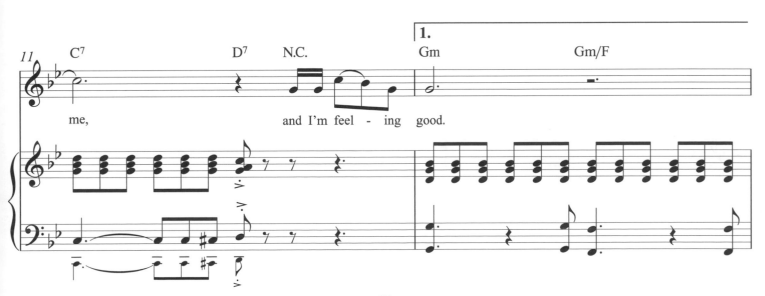

15

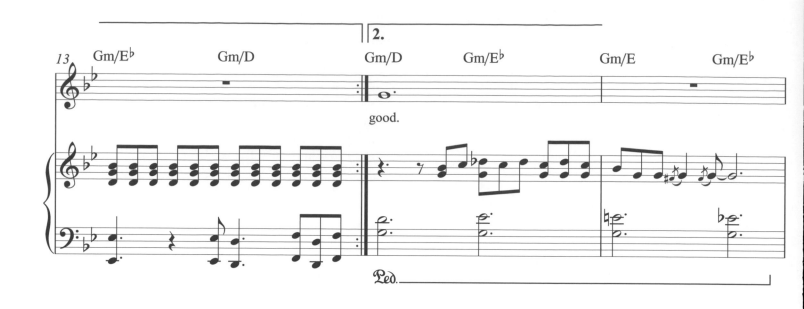

_____ in peace,_____ when the day is done_ and this old world_ is a new world,_ and a

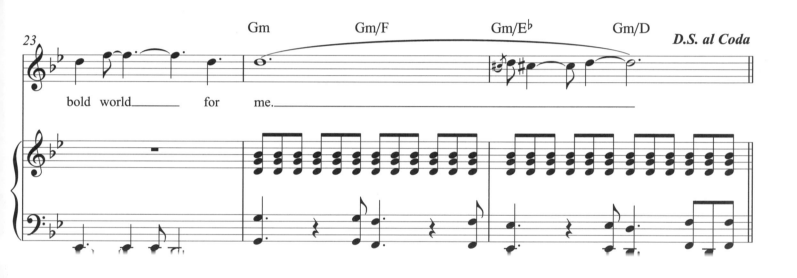

bold world_____ for me._____

D.S. al Coda

Gm   Gm/F   Gm/E♭   Gm/D

⊕ Coda

C⁷   A

me._____ Feel-ing good_____ ooh,_____

17

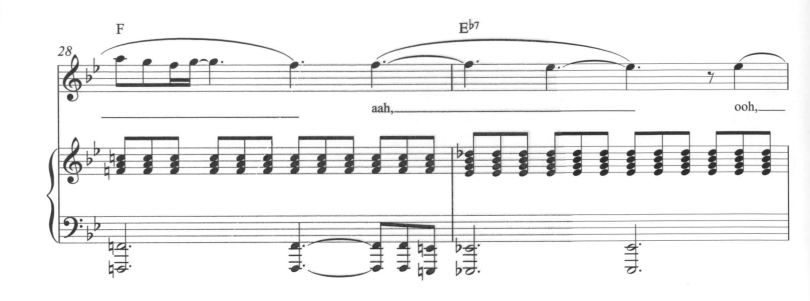

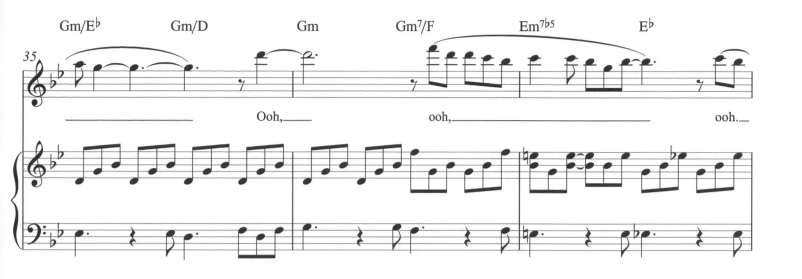

Ooh,_____ ooh,_____ ooh.__

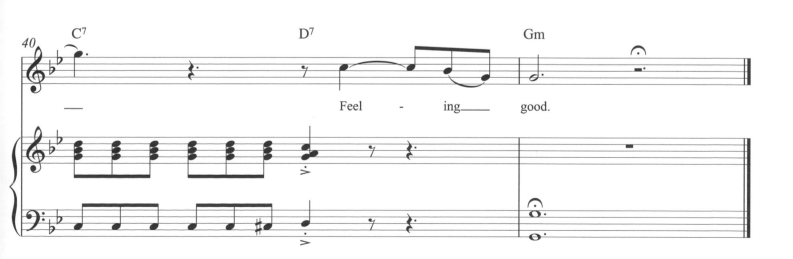

Feel - ing___ good.

FIELDS OF GOLD
Sting

'Fields Of Gold' is taken from *Ten Summoner's Tales*, Sting's fourth solo album, which was released in 1993. This song has been covered by numerous artists, the most popular being Eva Cassidy's version on her album *Live At Blues Alley*. Recorded in 1996, this was her final album before her tragic death aged 33.

This arrangement has a very playable and effective piano part. Keep the left-hand patterns rolling along in a relaxed but rhythmic manner to help create the mesmeric backing for the right hand chords and vocals. Try playing the left hand an octave lower to give extra depth or variation, perhaps for the second verse:

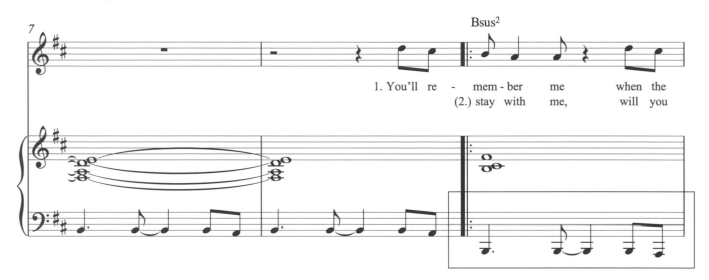

The dynamic level of this song should stay low throughout although you could bring out the instrumental melody a little in bars 40 to 47:

Keep the repeated end section relaxed and soft.

FIELDS OF GOLD

Words & Music by Sting

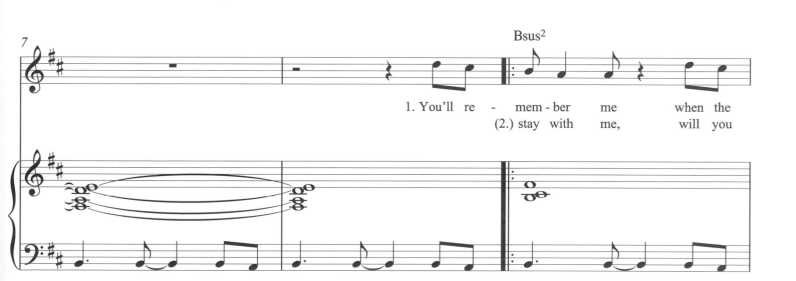

1. You'll re - mem - ber me when the
(2.) stay with me, when will you

but I swear_ in the days still left we'll walk_ in fields_ of gold.

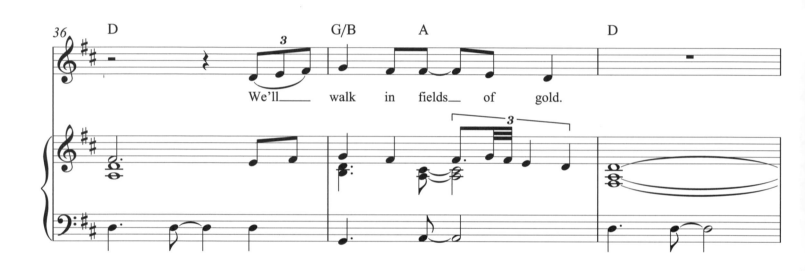

We'll_ walk in fields_ of gold.

24

HEAVEN
Bryan Adams

Bryan Adams wrote this song with Jim Vallance in 1983. It appeared on the *A Night In Heaven* soundtrack album and the *Reckless* album of 1984 and (as a single) reached No. 1 on the US Billboard Hot 100 in 1985. DJ Sammy and Yanou released a dance cover of 'Heaven' in 2002 with the Dutch artist Do on vocals. This arrangement is of the slow remix version and calls for some pianistic flair!

The sustain pedal really comes in useful in this piece, enabling you to keep the left-hand bass notes ringing whilst playing the arpeggio patterns above. It is marked at the start, *Con pedale*, and should be used throughout, at each chord change. *8va* means the passages under the bracket should be played an octave higher than written:

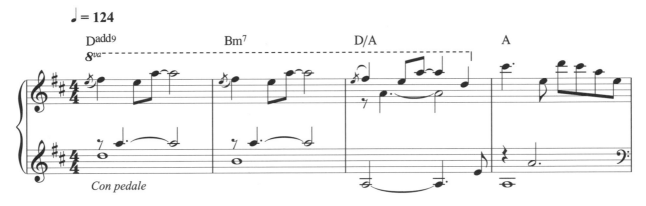

As a ballad the song should start relatively quietly and not start to build until the chorus in bar 29, but should reduce in volume again for the second verse. Bar 45 signals the start of the mid-section and a change of mood; the volume can really start to pick up here, ready to go back into the chorus:

The song ends quietly from bar 52 onwards, slowing towards the final arpeggiated chord.

HEAVEN

Words & Music by Bryan Adams & Jim Vallance

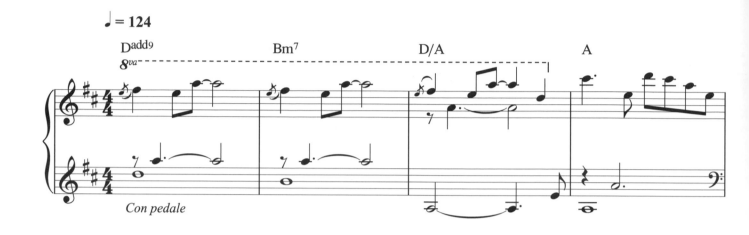

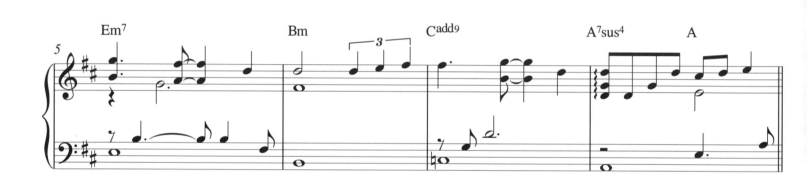

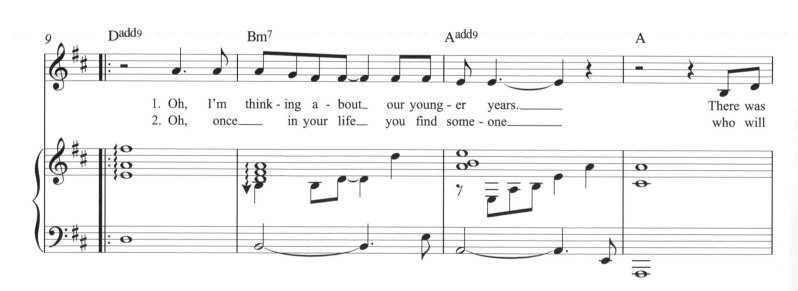

1. Oh, I'm think-ing a-bout our young-er years. There was
2. Oh, once in your life you find some-one who will

I KNOW HIM SO WELL
Elaine Paige and Barbara Dickson

Written by Tim Rice with music by ABBA's Björn Ulvaeus and Benny Andersson, 'I Know Him So Well' was first heard on the successful *Chess* album of 1984 sung by Elaine Paige and Barbara Dickson. *Chess* the musical opened in the West End in 1986 at the Prince Edward Theatre.

One of the best selling duets of all time (hence the two vocal staves), this arrangement includes the main melody in the right hand whilst the left hand provides the harmonic support as arpeggios for much of the time. This calls for judicious use of the sustain pedal; you want things to be smooth but not to all blur together. During the intro, it looks like there's a rest missing in the left hand part (bars 5 and 7). At these points the left hand should 'help out' the right by playing the bottom notes in the treble clef:

As it's a love song keep things smooth and gentle until bar 18 when the chorus needs to make a firm statement:

The same goes again in bar 37 for the second verse, and keep the energy level high until bar 52 when a quieter, more reflective mood takes over for the ending.

I KNOW HIM SO WELL

Words by Tim Rice
Music by Benny Andersson & Björn Ulvaeus

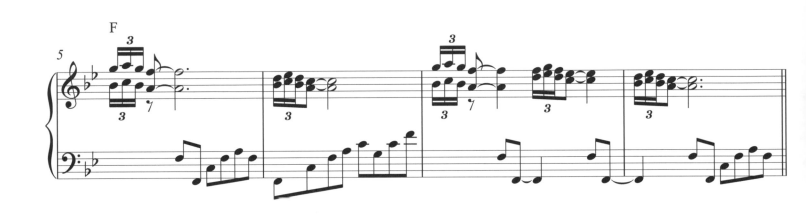

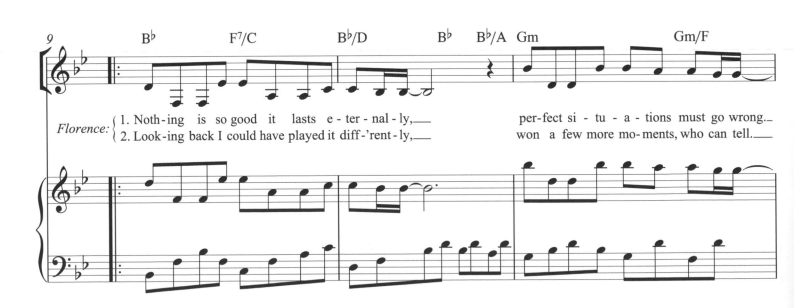

Florence: 1. Noth-ing is so good it lasts e-ter-nal-ly,___ per-fect si-tu-a-tions must go wrong...
2. Look-ing back I could have played it diff-'rent-ly,___ won a few more mo-ments, who can tell.___

But in the end he needs a lit-tle bit more than me, more___ se-

He needs his fan-ta-sy and free-dom.

- cu-ri-ty.   I know him so well.

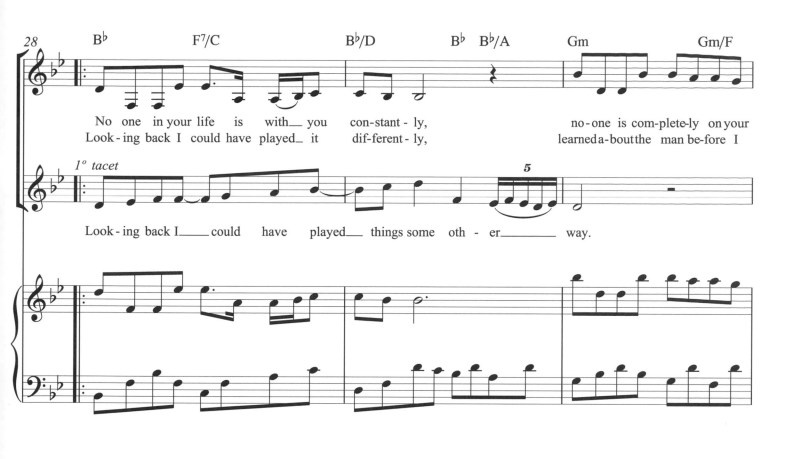

No one in your life is with you con-stant-ly, no-one is com-plete-ly on your
Look-ing back I could have played it dif-ferent-ly, learned a-bout the man be-fore I

Look-ing back I could have played things some oth-er way.

side. And though I move my world to be with him.
fell. But I was ev-er so much young-er then,

I was just a lit-tle care-less, may-be, I was so much young-er then,

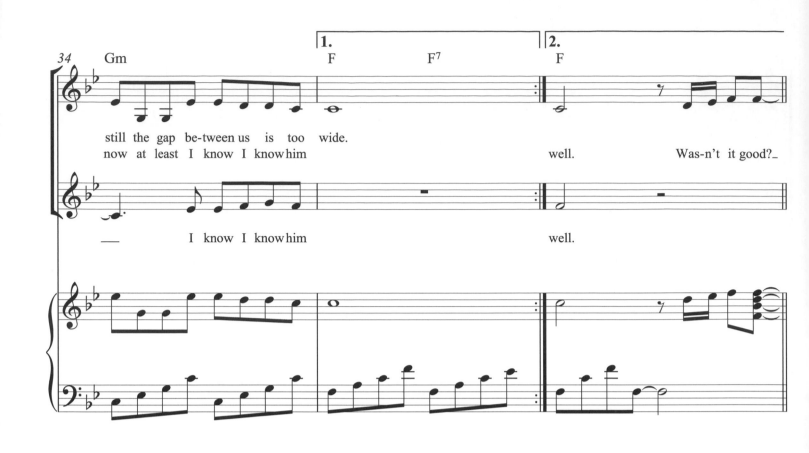

still the gap be-tween us is too wide.
now at least I know I know him

_____ I know I know him well.

_____ Was-n't he fine?_____ Is-n't it mad - ness he won't be mine?_

Oh, so good! Oh, so fine!_____ He won't be mine?_

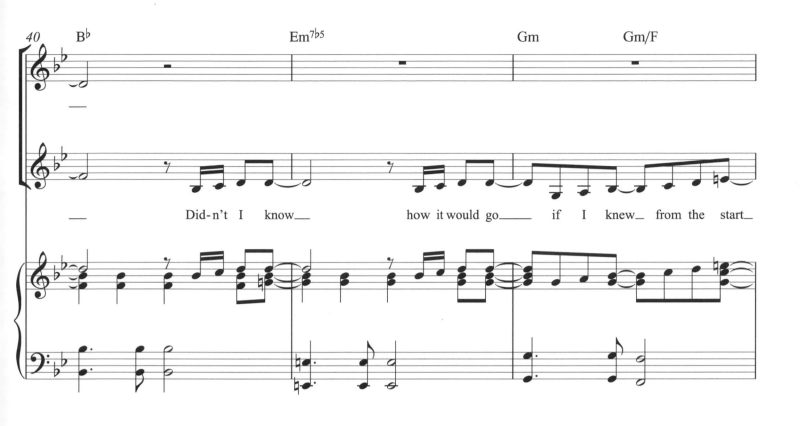

Did-n't I know_ how it would go_____ if I knew_ from the start_

Was-n't it good?_
why___ am I fall - ing a - part?____

Was-n't he fine?_____ He won't be mine?____

Is-n't it mad - ness he won't be mine?____ But

He needs his fan - ta - sy and

in the end he needs a lit-tle bit more than me, more____ se - cu - ri - ty.

41

MACK THE KNIFE
Robbie Williams

Written for their musical drama *The Threepenny Opera* in 1928 by Bertholt Brecht and Kurt Weill, this song has been transformed over the years to become a standard in the Swing repertoire. Many recording stars have performed this song, including Louis Armstrong, Bobby Darin, Franks Sinatra and Robbie Williams. This is an arrangement of the Robbie Williams version from his 2001 album *Swing When You're Winning*.

The right hand part has both the offbeat chords and the melody included but if you're playing this with a singer it's fine to leave the melody line out. Perhaps the trickiest thing in this piece is coping with the five key changes! This looks pretty daunting, but if you can master the first section up to bar 21 you should notice that each new section is virtually the same but moved up a half step:

At bar 15, you'll notice a bracket around the lower notes of the right hand part:

This indicates that these can be played with the left hand, as it's quite a stretch for the right hand alone!

The different artists who have performed this often put their own spin on the song. Try doing this yourself! Once you've got the hang of the chords and all the changes, the melody lends itself well to a little improvisation.

MACK THE KNIFE

Words by Bertolt Brecht
Music by Kurt Weill

back in town.____   I said____ Jen - ny

Di - ver,_____   old   Su - ky   Taw - dry,____

Spoken: Look out, Miss Lotte Lenya   and   old_____   Lu - cy   Brown;

yeah   the   line   forms_____   on____   the   right   babe,____

now that Mack - ie's

back in town.

Look out, old Mack - ie is back! Yeah!

MAD WORLD
Michael Andrews feat. Gary Jules

'Mad World' was written by Roland Orzabal and sung by Kurt Smith, who formed their band Tears For Fears in 1981. 'Mad World' appeared on their debut album *The Hurting*. In 2001 Michael Andrews and Gary Jules recorded their version of the song for the soundtrack to the movie *Donnie Darko*. In 2003 this recording reached No. 1 in the U.K. charts, two places higher than the original Tears For Fears version managed in the 1980s!

The minimalistic style of this piece makes the piano accompaniment relatively straightforward. There are virtually no dynamic changes in this song so it's best to start at a *mezzo piano* (moderately soft) level and remain there throughout. In the first verse (from bar 5), the right hand plays alone and is in the bass clef. If you're playing this as a solo piano piece, this can easily be played by the left hand, with the vocal melody in the right; otherwise, it changes to the treble clef in bar 21, which is the start of the chorus:

The left hand is added on the repeat, where it plays the simple cello line from the song:

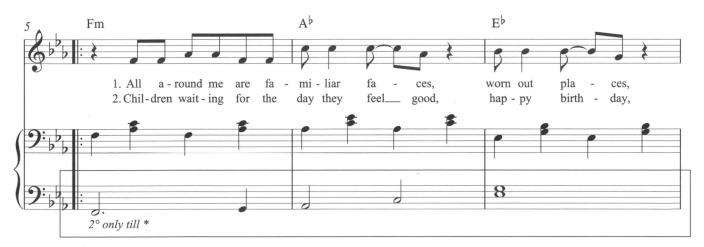

51

MAD WORLD

Words & Music by Roland Orzabal

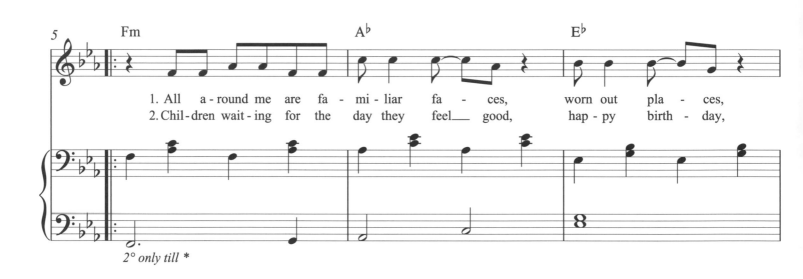

THE MAN WHO CAN'T BE MOVED
The Script

The Script released their self-titled debut album in 2008 and its second single, 'The Man Who Can't Be Moved' raced up the UK charts, finally peaking at No. 2. In 2012 it re-entered the charts after an airing on the TV show *The Voice*.

As it is mostly made up of four-bar patterns (as per the example below) this song should be relatively straightforward to learn. The piano accompaniment for this song is emulating a guitar so the sustain pedal will be really useful here to create the desired effect. Be sure to lift the pedal for each change of chord, e.g.:

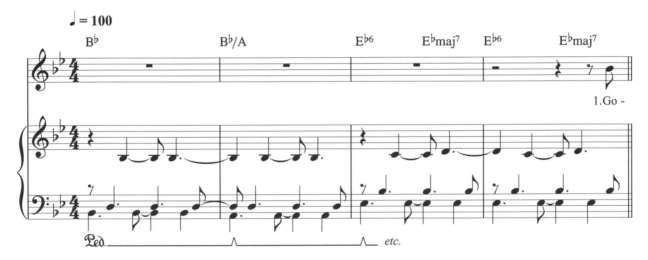

The first four bars are repeated right up to bar 21 when another four bar phrase takes over for the chorus. The middle section of this song starts at bar 42 with another, simpler four bar pattern followed by a two bar pattern ending on four bars of a C9 chord, leading nicely back into the chorus at bar 60:

This carries on till bar 69, where the song is ended by the repetition of the first four bars of verse one.

THE MAN WHO CAN'T BE MOVED

Words & Music by Andrew Frampton, Steve Kipner,
Mark Sheehan & Daniel O'Donoghue

1. Go - ing back to the cor - ner where I first saw you. Gon -

-na camp in my sleep-ing bag.__ I'm not gon-na move. Got some words on card-board, got

see me wait-ing for you___ on the corn-er of the street. So I'm not___ mov - ing.___

I'm not mov - ing.___

I'm not mov - ing.___ I'm not mov - ing.___

MY IMMORTAL
Evanescence

'My Immortal' is considered to be the most successful single by the American rock group Evanescence. Taken from their 2003 album *Fallen*, the single version was a massive hit in more than ten countries. The song has been used extensively in the media including film and TV, notably in promos for the final episodes of *Friends*.

This arrangement is based on the album version of the song. Start quietly and build the volume towards the chorus (bar 17) which should really take off!

After the chorus, however, you should bring the volume down during the first time bar, so the second verse will be played at the same volume as the first. Bar 30 should go up another level so you can really pump out the left-hand bass notes, maybe doubling the octave here:

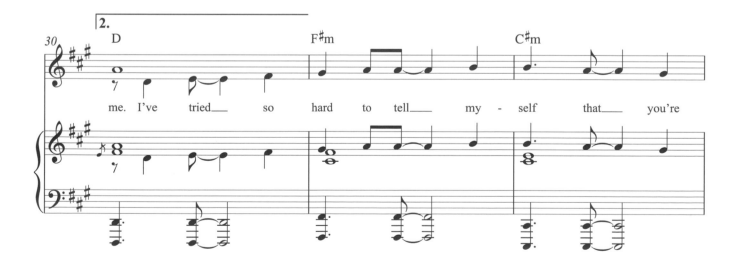

The coda sees the song return to the gentle feel of the intro with a *rit.* in bar 49.

MY IMMORTAL

Words & Music by Ben Moody, Amy Lee & David Hodges

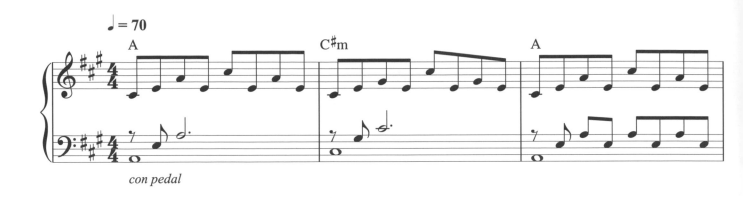

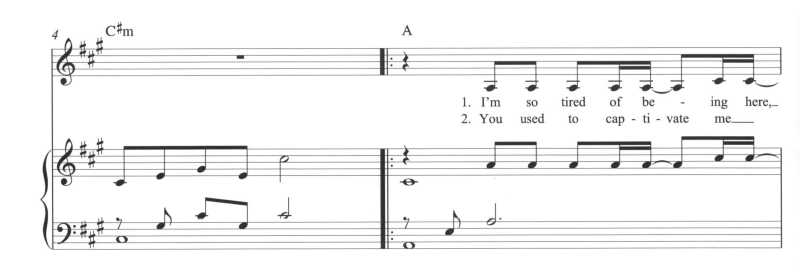

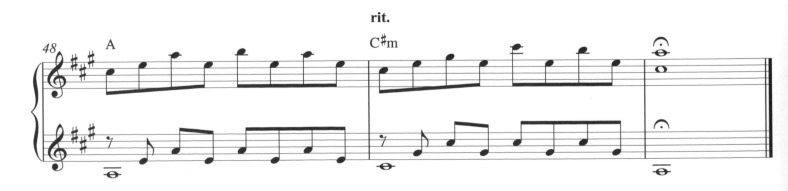

RULE THE WORLD
Take That

'Rule The World' is taken from Take That's album *Beautiful World* which was released in 2007. This song featured in the closing credits of the film *Stardust* and was later released as a single, reaching No. 2 in the UK charts.

This song has a pretty straightforward piano accompaniment. The four-note chords starting in bar 14 may prove challenging for some but leaving out the bottom note at this point will make things a lot easier without losing too much of the desired effect:

Verse 2 has a heavier feel to it, which is indicated by the eighth notes in the left hand; the first time round, only the top whole notes are played:

Crescendo through bars 12 and 13 into the chorus and try to make the sixteenth notes that start in bar 27 as even as possible.

RULE THE WORLD

**Words & Music by Mark Owen, Gary Barlow,
Jason Orange & Howard Donald**

RUN
Leona Lewis

'Run' made it into the top 5 of the UK charts in 2004. It was taken from the third album released by Snow Patrol, *Final Straw*. The song made it back into the charts in 2008 after Leona Lewis performed it frequently on radio and TV. Her version became the UK's fastest selling download-only song.

This very pianistic accompaniment to the Leona Lewis version will benefit from use of the sustain pedal in the sixteenth note passages, which will help to keep a smooth and relaxed feel to the piano part. This especially applies in the instrumental/vocal *ad lib.* section starting in bar 39:

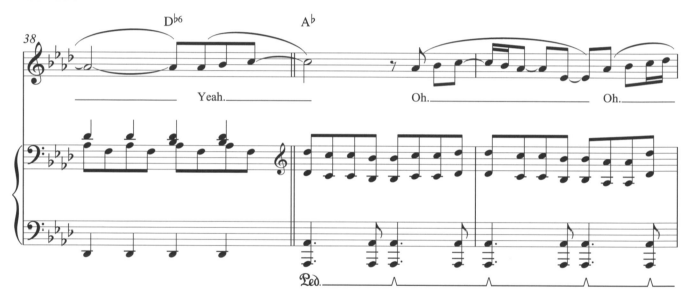

The song should build gradually in volume and intensity, dropping right down for the ending which starts in bar 49:

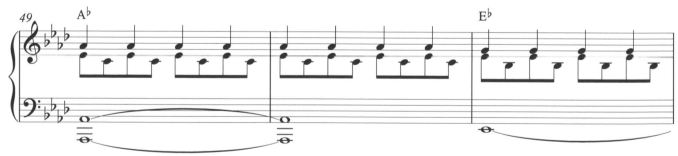

Note that much of the right hand is in the bass clef. This piano part is well worth mastering and actually sounds great on its own!

RUN

Words & Music by Gary Lightbody, Jonathan Quinn,
Mark McClelland, Nathan Connolly & Iain Archer

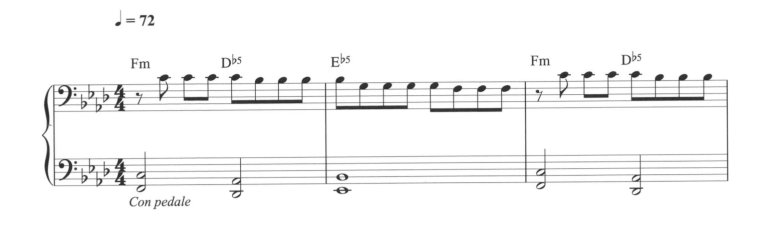

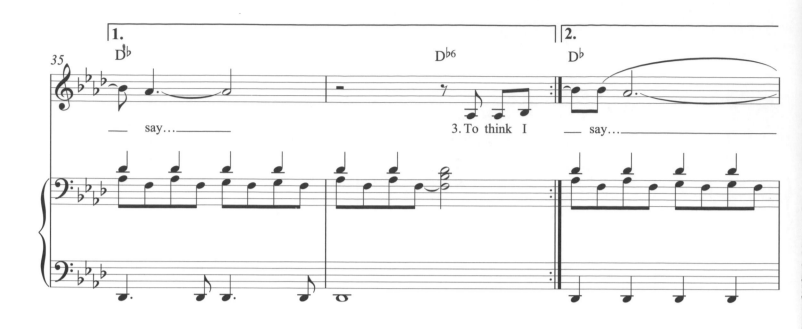

say…   3. To think I   say…

Yeah.   Oh.   Oh.

Oh.   Oh.   Oh.

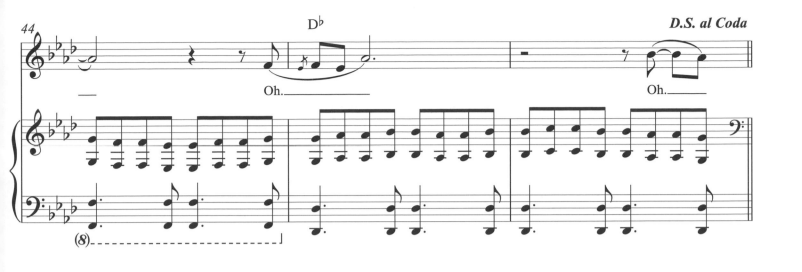

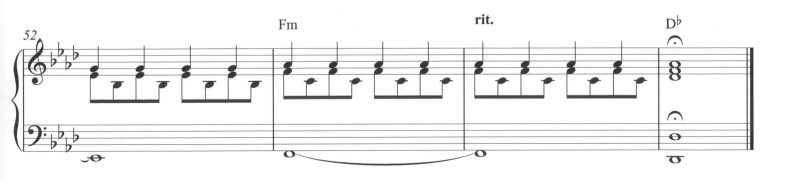

THE SCIENTIST
Coldplay

Coldplay's ballad 'The Scientist' was recorded for their second studio album *A Rush Of Blood To The Head* in 2002 and released as a single in that same year. Although it didn't achieve great chart success it has, over time, proved to be one of the band's best-loved songs.

Keep the repeated eighth notes in the left hand nice and even to help create the meditative, hypnotic feel this song should have. To help increase the intensity of the second verse you could double the notes in the left hand an octave lower at the repeat in bar 9:

The instrumental section beginning at bar 43 can be heavier again. Make sure the sixteenth notes in the right hand come through clearly at this point, as they add interest to the repetitive eighth notes:

This heavier feel continues up to the final three bars, which should be much softer.

THE SCIENTIST

**Words & Music by Guy Berryman, Chris Martin,
Jon Buckland & Will Champion**

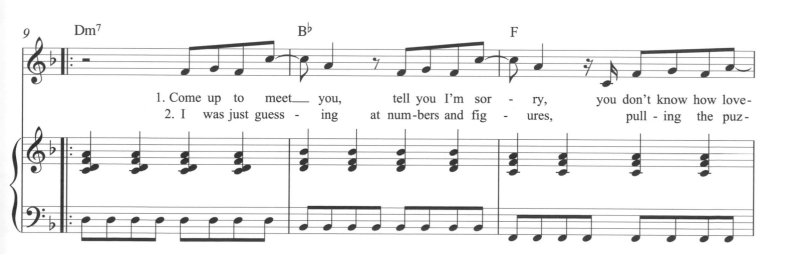

1. Come up to meet___ you, tell you I'm sor - ry, you don't know how love-
2. I was just guess - ing at num-bers and fig - ures, pull - ing the puz-

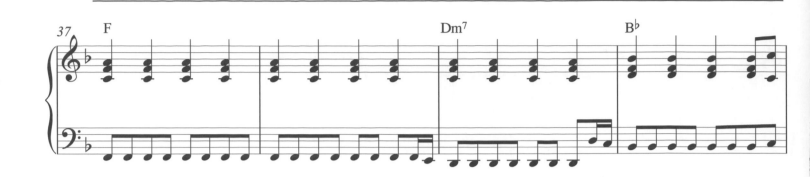

SOMEONE LIKE YOU
Adele

'Someone Like You' was written by Adele and her co-writer Dan Wilson for her second album *21*. This is a deeply emotional song about a broken relationship. A huge international hit, 'Someone Like You' has been covered by many artists, including Katy Perry and the *Glee* cast, and has also been used in several film soundtracks.

The structure of this song looks quite confusing at first. Listen to the song while looking through the piano part before you start playing it through, so you know exactly where to go at each section. Particularly look out for 'first time only' sections which indicated the passage under the bracket should be skipped on the repeat:

Bar 23 is where the song picks up intensity and volume. Bar 40 sees the sixteenth notes take a break, but the sustain pedal is still useful here to help give you more time to find the next chord:

SOMEONE LIKE YOU

Words & Music by Daniel Wilson & Adele Adkins

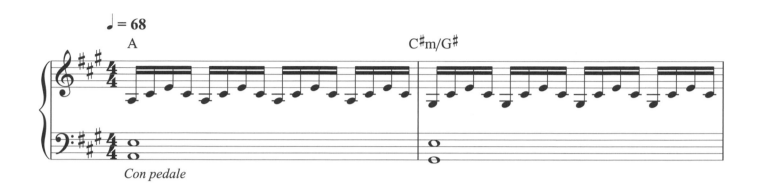

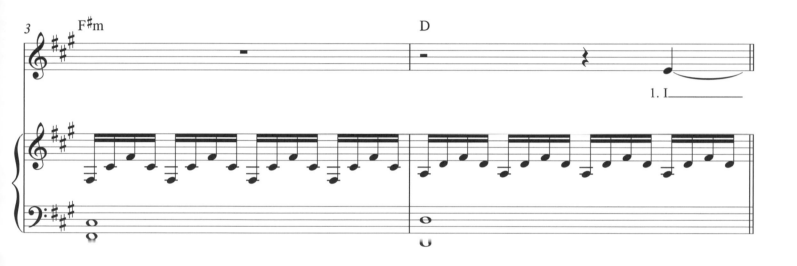

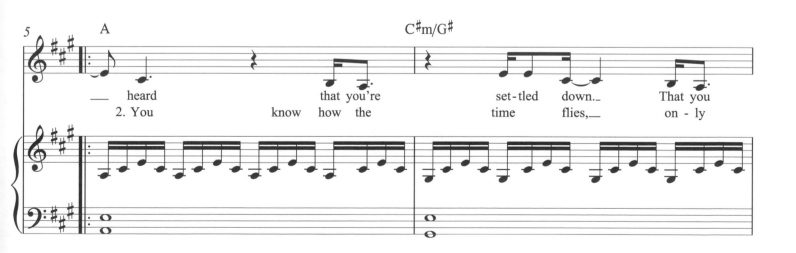

A THOUSAND YEARS

Christina Perri

'A Thousand Years' was written by Christina Perri and David Hodges for the 2011 movie *The Twilight Saga: Breaking Dawn Part 1*. Another version was recorded for the second part of *Breaking Dawn*, featuring the vocals of Steve Kazee. It reached No. 11 in the U.K. charts and was performed on the TV show *The X Factor*.

This song needs to float along, so keeping the left hand smooth and unobtrusive is a priority. The two against three pattern in the left hand is the most difficult problem to overcome in this piece. Try practising this part on its own nice and slowly; if you break it down, essentially your left hand is playing this rhythm (count 1, 2 and 3, 1, 2 and 3 etc.):

Count: 1   2   &   3,   1   2   &   3,   1   2   &   3,   *etc.*

Playing the upper part of the bass stave with the right hand does make things easier most of the time but missing the odd note out doesn't matter as long as the lower part keeps on moving. Start quietly and build slowly to the instrumental break in bar 23. Bar 27, where the vocals re-enter, is a softer section up until bar 35, where the intensity of the song is raised again with the addition of octaves in the left hand:

Bar 39 to the end is as quiet as the beginning of the song.

A THOUSAND YEARS

Words & Music by David Hodges & Christina Perri

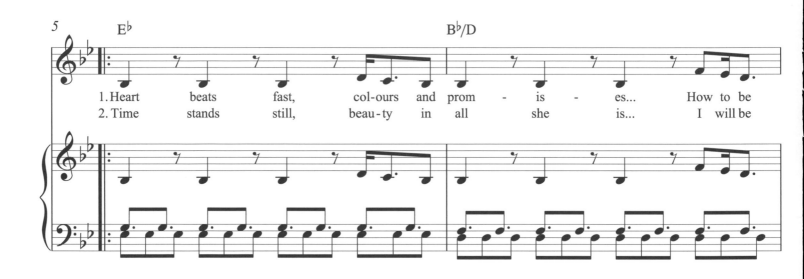

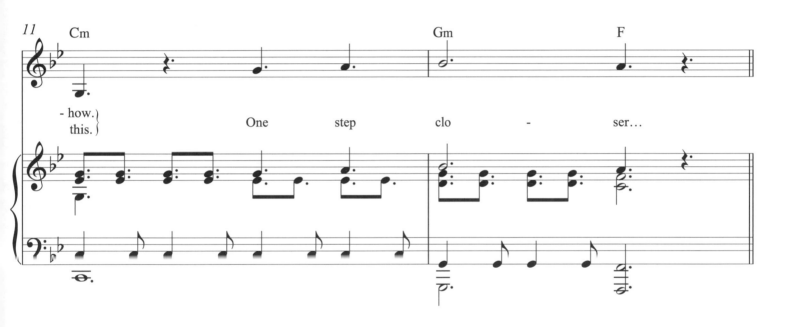

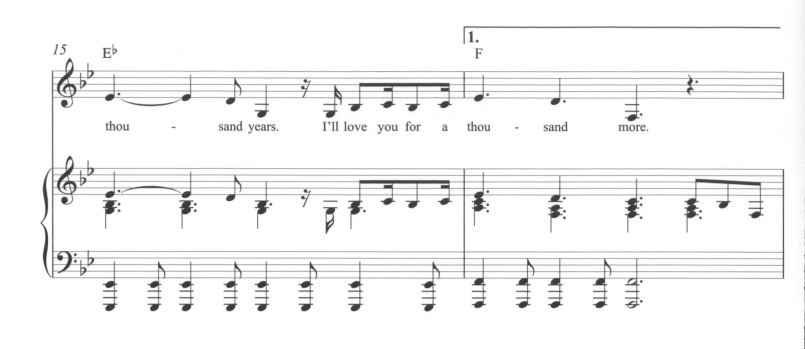

thou - sand years. I'll love you for a thou - sand more.

thou - sand more. And

all a long I be-lieved I would find you. Time has brought your heart to me. I have loved_ you for a

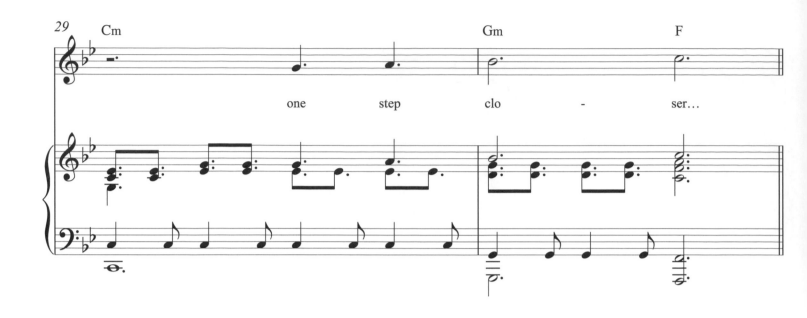

one step clo - ser...

I have died ev-'ry day wait-ing for you. Darl-ing don't be a-fraid, I have loved_ you for a

thou - sand years. I'll love you for a thou - sand more. And

WARWICK AVENUE
Duffy

Welsh soul singer Duffy released her single 'Warwick Avenue' in 2008. Taken from the album *Rockferry*, which was voted Best British Album at the 2009 Brit Awards, 'Warwick Avenue' spent six weeks in the top ten of UK singles charts, peaking at No. 3. Warwick Avenue is a tube station on the Bakerloo line of the London Underground.

The first four bars of the piano accompaniment are to be played *mezzo piano* and are repeated right up to bar 19, so once you've mastered this passage it should make things easier:

The chorus, starting at bar 21, needs to be a little heavier. The right hand chords starting at bar 38 should bounce along. Bring out the melody in the instrumental section starting in bar 48 by putting slightly more emphasis on the top note of the right hand part when playing:

Drop the level right down again for the ending from bar 55 onwards.

WARWICK AVENUE

Words & Music by James Hogarth, Aimee Duffy
& Francis Eg White

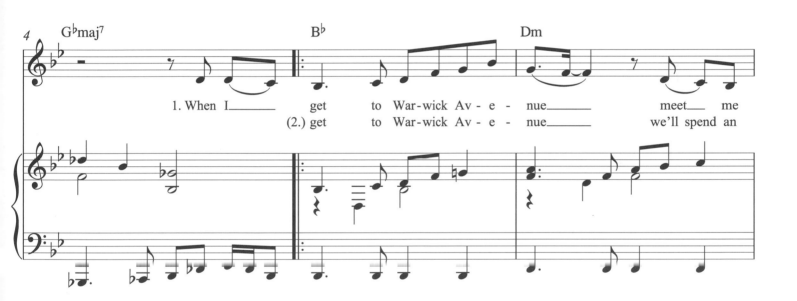

1. When I_____ get to War-wick Av-e - nue_____ meet___ me
(2.) get to War-wick Av-e - nue_____ we'll spend an

by the en - trance of_____ the tube. We can___ talk things o - ver__ a lit-tle
hour but no more than__ two. Our on - ly chance to speak once

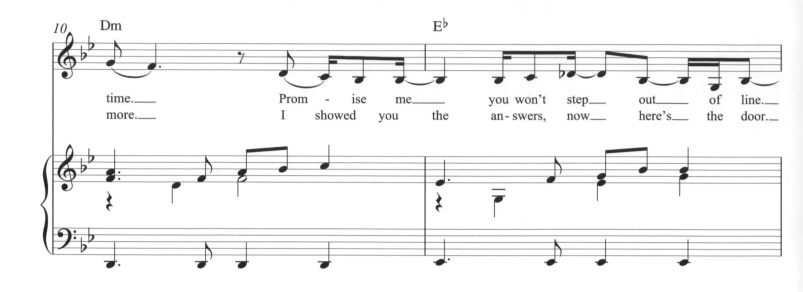

time.____ Prom - ise me____ you won't step____ out____ of line.____
more.____ I showed you the an - swers, now____ here's____ the door.____

____ When I_____ get to War-wick Av - e - nue____ please_ drop_
____ When I_____ get to War-wick Av - e - nue____ I'll tell you

1° only

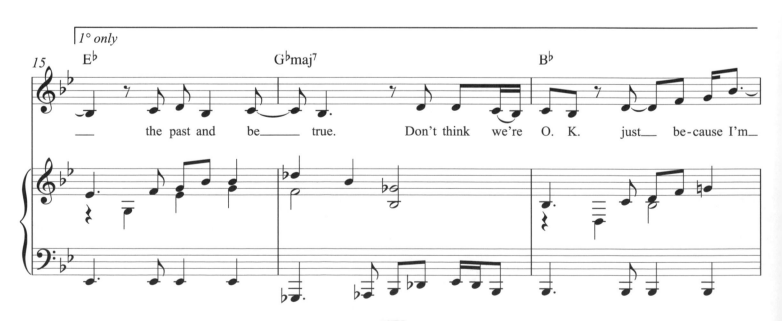

____ the past and be_____ true. Don't think we're O. K. just____ be-cause I'm

YOUR SONG

Ellie Goulding

This Elton John classic was first released in 1970 and has been covered by a number of artists. This version is from Ellie Gouldin's 2010 album *Bright Lights*. She performed it at Prince William and Catherine Middleton's wedding reception.

The melody can be played quite loosely over the main pulse in the left hand. Make the triplets nice and lazy to differentiate them from the groups of sixteenth notes. At bar 20 a heavier feel is created with the introduction of octaves in the left hand.

Bar 27 is in 5/4 but is nothing to fear as long as the left hand eighth notes are kept moving in time. Bar 28 to 35 is a more reflective section in 3/4 time. Try spreading the right hand chords here to lighten the mood:

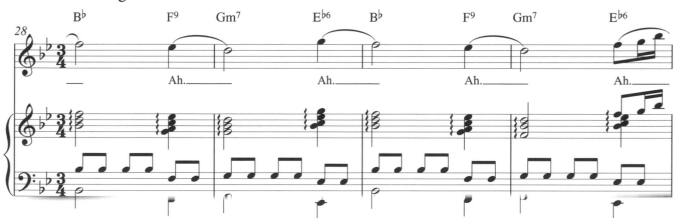

This is a neatly structured song that should gradually build from the third verse until the fermata (pause) in bar 36:

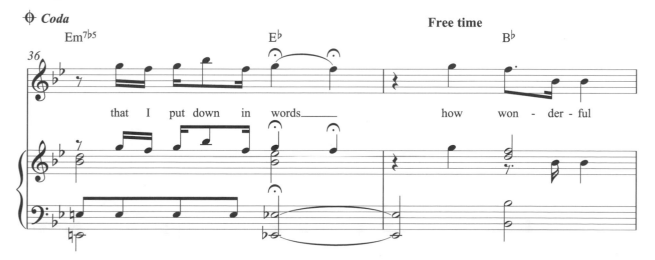

The final three bars are in 'Free time' which means you can really do whatever you want with the tempo!

YOUR SONG

Words & Music by Elton John & Bernie Taupin

8vb throughout

1. It's a lit - tle bit fun - ny,   this feel - ing in - side.___
2. So ex - cuse me for - get - ting,   but these things I do.___

I'm not one of those___ who___ can   eas - i - ly hide.___
See, I've for - got - ten___ if   they're green or they're blue.___

I don't have much mon - ey   but boy, if I did
An - y - way the thing is,   what I real - ly mean,

HOW TO DOWNLOAD YOUR MUSIC TRACKS

1. Carefully remove your Download Card from the inside back cover of this book.

2. On the back of the card is your unique access code. Enter this at www.musicsalesdownloads.com

TO REDEEM THIS CARD VISIT
www.musicsalesdownloads.com

ENTER ACCESS CODE:

XXXXXXXXX

Download Cards are powered by Dropcards.
User must accept terms at dropcards.com/terms
which are adopted by The Music Sales Group.
Not reedemable for cash. Void where prohibited or restricted by law.

DCARD1006478

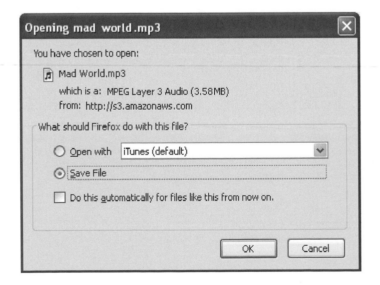

3. Follow the instructions to save your files to your computer*. That's it!

*Appearance of download manager will vary depending upon operating system and web browser.
In case of difficulty when downloading files, please contact dropcards.com/help
Card missing? Please contact music@musicsales.co.uk